# BUILDING A ROCK-SOLID PARTNERSHIP WITH YOUR BOARD

## A Real-Life, Practical Guidebook for Nonprofit and Public CEOs

By
### Doug Eadie

President & CEO
Doug Eadie & Company

A Governance Edge® Publication

A publication of
Governance Edge®
Doug Eadie & Company
3 Sunny Point Terrace
Oldsmar, FL 34677

Phone: 800-209-7652
Email: info@GovernanceEdge.com
A complete listing of books and CDs by Doug Eadie is available
at www.DougEadie.com.

ISBN  978-0-9798894-2-4
Library of Congress Control Number:  2008906095

**Library of Congress Subject Headings:**
Nonprofit Organizations–Management
Boards of directors

FOR MY SISTER AND BROTHER-IN-LAW

KAY SUE AND JIM NAGLE

# TABLE OF CONTENTS

# FOREWORD

I LEARNED EARLY in my twenty-three-year tenure as president and CEO of the Council for Urban Economic Development and, since a merger in 2001, the International Economic Development Council, that one of my top CEO priorities—and challenges— was to build and maintain a really solid partnership with my Board of Directors. I recognized that the kind of governing that makes a significant difference—what Doug Eadie calls "high-impact" governing—depended on my working as a close partner with my Board. This wasn't just altruism at work. I also knew that such a partnership was critical to my long-term success— and longevity!—as a CEO. I'm pleased to report that the IEDC Board of Directors and I work together as a cohesive "Strategic Governing Team," providing the leadership that has enabled IEDC to thrive in these changing, challenging times.

I also learned early in my CEO career that really practical, detailed guidance on building close, positive, and productive board-CEO partnerships wasn't readily available in the non-profit or public literature—at least not guidance that had been thoroughly tested in real-life situations. So I found myself doing a lot of trial-and-error learning in those days, and, as you can imagine, I now and then got pretty banged up in the process. So I'm delighted that Doug Eadie has written *Building a Rock-Solid Partnership With Your Board.* This is the kind of down-to-earth, practical resource I could have used a quarter-century ago!

*Building a Rock-Solid Partnership With Your Board* is a plain-spoken, easy-to-read guidebook that is chock-full of practical partnership-building techniques that you can put to immediate use in your organization. The advice and counsel that Doug Eadie offers isn't theoretical. It has been battle-tested in his work over the past twenty-five years with more than 500 real-life boards and CEOs.

I strongly recommend that you keep *Building a Rock-Solid Partnership With Your Board* close at hand and consult it often as you and your board journey together on the governing road.

Jeffrey A. Finkle, President & CEO
International Economic Development Council
Washington, DC

# ACKNOWLEDGMENTS

OVER THE PAST TWENTY-FIVE YEARS, I've collaborated with hundreds of board-savvy CEOs in developing their boards' governing capacity and building really solid partnerships with their boards. They have been my teachers as well as my colleagues, enriching my understanding of the governing "business" and sharing their tricks of the partnership-building trade. Among my closest CEO colleagues in recent years who have significantly contributed to the practical wisdom in this guidebook are: Steve Bland, CEO of the Port Authority of Allegheny County; Ronnie Bryant, president & CEO of the Charlotte Regional Partnership; Sue Buchholtz, president & CEO of the Pinellas Association of Retarded Citizens; Jerry Custin, president & CEO of the Upper Tampa Bay Regional Chamber of Commerce; Paul Dugan, superintendent of the Washoe County School District; Jeff Finkle, president & CEO of the International Economic Development Council; Virginia Jacko, president & CEO of the Miami Lighthouse for the Blind and Visually Impaired, Inc.; Linda Kloss, CEO of the American Health Information Management Association; James McGuirk, executive director & CEO of Astor Home for Children; Robert Nelson, president & CEO of the National Coffee Association; Pamela Shea, superintendent of the Teton County School District #1; Peter Varga, executive director and CEO of the Interurban Transit Partnership; and Lana Vukovljak, CEO of the American Association of Diabetes Educators.

Other colleagues who provided insightful comments on the manuscript of this guidebook are: Janegale Boyd, president & CEO of the Florida Association of Homes and Services for the Aging; Skardon Bliss, executive director of the Florida Council of Independent Schools; Jane Gallucci, member of the Pinellas County Board of Education and immediate past president of the National School Boards Association; Amparo Gonzalez, president of the Board of Directors of the American Association of Diabetes Educators; Jim Harnish, Senior Pastor of Hyde Park United Methodist Church; Paul Houston, executive director of the American Association of School Administrators; Steven Marcus, president & CEO of the Health Foundation of South Florida; Paul Martodam, CEO of Catholic Charities in Phoenix; David Nacht, chair of the Board of Directors of the Ann Arbor Transportation Authority; and Genny Rose, executive director of the Arizona Association of Homes and Housing for the Aging.

Cathy Ordiway, Technical Director of Doug Eadie & Company, provided several suggestions for improving the manuscript of this book, and Angela Ashe, Administrative Director of Doug Eadie & Company, handled myriad administrative details, allowing me to focus on the writing task.

My children, Jennifer and William, took time from their demanding law school schedules to help in refining this book's key concepts, drawing on their extensive public and nonprofit executive experience, and my sister and close friend, Kay Sue Nagle, provided thoughtful input during my preparation of the manuscript.

Finally, I am indebted to my best friend, esteemed professional colleague, and wife, Barbara Carlson Krai, for her unconditional love and unwavering support, without which my writing task would have been immeasurably more difficult, if not impossible. I am also deeply appreciative of Barbara's shouldering the full burden of overseeing the ongoing renovation of both our home and offices, leaving me free to concentrate on this guidebook.

Of course, I alone am responsible for any flaws *Building a Rock-Solid Partnership With Your Board* might possess.

Doug Eadie
Tampa Bay, Florida

# INTRODUCTION:
# THE FIVE KEYS TO A ROCK-SOLID PARTNERSHIP

HOW DO YOU KNOW that you're a really board-savvy CEO and a master of the governing "business"? Twenty-five years of work with more than 500 nonprofit and public organizations in diverse fields—including association management, education, health care, aging, transportation, and economic development—have taught me that the surest sign that your governing IQ tops the charts is a rock-solid partnership with your board. Real-life experience—not theory—has taught me that the CEOs who have built this kind of partnership with their boards tend to be far more successful as leaders and executive managers, and they also tend to be longer-tenured than their less board-savvy peers. Keeping your working relationship with your board really healthy—close, positive, productive, and enduring—is no small challenge, in light of the inevitable stresses and strains at the top in any nonprofit or public organization in these always changing, challenging times. The board-CEO partnership is always quite fragile and can erode alarmingly fast if not systematically managed and constantly nurtured. And you should always keep in mind that even if you do a stellar job of handling important technical functions as a CEO, your partnership with you board can unravel over nontechnical relationship issues that you might not have been aware were a problem.

## PAYING ATTENTION TO THE HUMAN DIMENSION

I'll never forget, years ago, walking into the office of a CEO I was working with and finding him slumped over his desk. "For heaven's sake, what's wrong?" I asked. Without saying a word, he handed me an evaluation form that his board had reviewed with him earlier that morning. It was one of those checklists that ask evaluators to rate the CEO on his or her mastery of various functions, such as financial management and strategic planning. As I went down the list, I was struck by the high scores on every item and puzzled by the CEO's obvious depression. Then I came to the section at the end reserved for comments. What it said in so many words was: "You do a really great job of handling the critical functions, but it's time for us to part company, since working with you is so unsatisfying. We're an audience for your technically superb work (You're always right!), and that's not enough. You obviously aren't very interested in how creative our involvement is in making critical decisions, so you should take your brand of leadership elsewhere." He was gone a few weeks later.

I wish I could say that the example I just shared with you is truly extraordinary, but while it's certainly dramatic, it's not all that rare in my experience. Over the years I've been impressed by how critical a CEO's management of the psychological and emotional (what from this point on I will call the "human") dimension of the board-CEO partnership is. My quarter-century of work with hundreds of nonprofit and public organizations of all shapes and sizes has taught me that you, the CEO, can do 99 percent of your job extremely well but come to grief over a psychological/emotional issue you didn't even recognize as a problem. That's the reason I wrote this second book for Governance Edge. My intent in writing *Building a Rock-Solid Partnership With Your Board* is to provide you with detailed, practical guidance on handling the human dimension of your relationship with your board. You can think of this as a companion piece with my first Governance Edge book, *Meeting the Governing Challenge*, which describes the key elements of my High-Impact Governing Model: the general characteristics of "board-savvy" CEOs; the board's governing role and work; board standing committees; the board's management of itself as a governing body; and executive team support for the governing function.

## FIVE KEYS TO HANDLING THE HUMAN DIMENSION

If you are a CEO—whether your title is chief executive, president, executive director, general manager, or superintendent—who wants to beef up your governing "emotional IQ" in the interest of a stronger partnership with your board, this is the book for you. I describe five keys—tricks of the governing trade—that you can put to work immediately in handling the human dimension of your partnership with your board:

**1. Bring the right mindset to the governing arena.**

To be successful in building a really close, productive partnership with the board, the CEO has to start off on the right foot, seeing his or her board as a precious asset and the CEO as the point person in developing this asset. The CEO can't afford to be over-controlling or defensive in approaching his or her board, but should welcome and celebrate board empowerment.

**2. Make your board chair a close ally.**

The board chair is, by position, one of the CEO's pre-eminent stakeholders and a potential champion for CEO leadership initiatives. The board-savvy CEO takes the initiative, turning his or her board chair into an ally by, among other things, reaching detailed agreement on the basic division of leadership labor between the two of them, doing everything feasible to ensure the chair's success as leader of the board, and helping the chair to accomplish his or her professional aims.

**3. Turn your board members into strong owners.**

Owners make good colleagues and partners, and feelings of ownership breed commitment. Audiences might admire finished staff work, and even bless it, but no really board-savvy CEO would count on that kind of shallow commitment lasting much past the next crisis that the CEO and board have got to cope with. Board-savvy CEOs do whatever they can to turn their board members into strong owners of their governing work, by such means as ensuring the success of board standing committee chairs and designing creative, proactive board involvement into such critical processes as strategic planning, budgeting, and performance monitoring.

### 4. Make work more interesting and enjoyable.
Governing is complex, demanding work that can grind even the most committed and passionate board members down, killing their enthusiasm and eroding the board-CEO partnership. The CEO needs to pay attention to ways of making the governing experience easier, more interesting and even fun for board members. Board-savvy CEOs have employed such techniques as using creative graphics in performance reporting, spotlighting programs at board meetings, raising board members' sights above the day-to-day grind, and building informal, personal interaction into the governing process.

### 5. Put a well-designed CEO evaluation process in place.
Many boards avoid—or don't do a very good job of—evaluating their CEO, but a well-designed CEO evaluation process is one of the most powerful ways to keep the board-CEO partnership healthy. The major steps in an effective evaluation process are to charge a specific board committee with the responsibility, to reach agreement on a set of detailed CEO-specific performance targets that relate to the CEO's individual value-added, and to use the evaluation process as a vehicle for identifying relationship issues and coming up with initiatives to address them.

## UNIVERSALLY APPLICABLE

I know that some of you reading this guidebook will, at one point or another, sit back and say to yourself: "This sounds like really great advice—for an organization blessed with lots of staff and a big budget—but everyone in my ten-person shop is already up to their eyeballs in work, and we couldn't possibly apply what Doug is recommending in our organization." In response, let me assure you that you definitely can. I know that you can apply the five keys in any organization, from a neighborhood development corporation with 2½ staff to a retirement community or school district with more than 500 employees. That's what my quarter century of real-life experience in working with hundreds of nonprofit and public organizations of all shapes and sizes, engaged in a wide variety of fields and functions, has taught me. Of course, with fewer staff, you will probably need to slow down the pace a bit so you don't get overextended, but there's nothing you'll read in the following pages that you can't put to good use in building the kind of board-CEO partnership that you've got to have to thrive in today's world.

## KEY #1:
## BRING THE RIGHT MINDSET TO THE GOVERNING ARENA

THE BOARD-SAVVIEST CEOs I've worked with over my quarter century in the governing arena—the ones who have built and maintained really rock-solid partnerships with their boards—have brought a particular mindset to engaging with their boards in the governing arena. These consummate partnership builders agree on the following four critical points:

•**They see their board—and the work of governing—as one of their preeminent leadership responsibilities and a top-tier CEO priority, deserving their serious time and attention.** They therefore make the effort to become real experts in the complex, rapidly evolving field of nonprofit and public governance.

•**They passionately want—and enthusiastically celebrate—the kind of board leadership that makes a real difference.** They are aficionados of board empowerment who don't obsess about the dangers of board micromanagement or waste time and energy trying to keep their boards under control.

•**They see as one of their preeminent CEO responsibilities helping their boards to become higher-impact governing bodies.** Far from sitting back waiting for their boards to figure out themselves how to get better at governing, or whining about inadequate board governing performance, they don the Chief Board Capacity Builder cap and aggressively promote their board's development.

•**They view governing as a team sport, involving a close partnership between the board and CEO,** and they know that it doesn't make sense to try to draw a hard and fast

17

line between the "pure" governing work of the board and the "pure" executive management work they and their staff do. Board-savvy CEOs know that in the real world, the division of governing labor between the board and CEO will evolve over time as circumstances change and is a matter of creative negotiation, rather than rule making.

When a really board-savvy CEO looks at a board, he or she doesn't see an adversary to be contained or a threat to be countered; rather, what the CEO sees is:

- A precious organizational asset, consisting of members' experience, knowledge, creativity, energy and commitment, expertise, a network of external relationships, and political clout.

- And a wonderful opportunity to ensure that this precious asset is put to full use in governing at a high-level—in the ultimate interest of organizational effectiveness and growth.

When they look at a board, these board-savvy CEOs don't see a glass half-empty; in their eyes it's full to the brim!

## SAD TO SAY

Unfortunately, many, if not most, nonprofit and public CEOs I've observed over the years have brought lots of negative baggage to the boardroom. They've tended to see boards from a defensive perspective as a damage-control challenge, needing to be closely watched and controlled to ensure that their tentacles don't grab hold of functions that "rightly" belong to the CEO and executive team. The we-they syndrome is alive and well with these defensive CEOs, who feel quite comfortable, thank you, with the notion of clear boundaries separating "policy making," as they tend to call the board's work, from "policy execution," which they see as their turf. Bringing this essentially negative and defensive attitude to their work with the board, these CEOs have, in my experience, more often than not missed valuable opportunities to build close, positive partnerships with their boards and have found themselves moving on to other jobs when the relationship eventually wears out.

Allow me to share a real-life example of one of these un-board-savvy CEOs at work.

Not long ago I was chatting with the chief executive of a medium-sized association in the health care field about the nature of the board-CEO partnership. When we began discussing how the board and CEO might work together on the planning front, I asked her: "So, how have you involved your board members proactively and creatively in the budget preparation process so that they can feel stronger ownership of, and take satisfaction in, their governing work? I know it isn't easy, since budgets are largely administrative documents without a lot of room for intensive board involvement." "Well, Doug," she responded, "I'm not sure what you mean by 'creative,' but I don't think I could do much more than I am without inviting micromanagement." She went on to say that her process was to present the board's planning committee with a completed budget document two months before the beginning of the next fiscal year. The committee would then thumb through this finished budget, asking for clarification and occasionally suggesting adjustments in line items.

"I guess you'd call my approach 'review and react'," she pointed out, "and I'm not about to open Pandora's Box by inviting them any further into the process." When I asked her how satisfied her board members appeared to be with their involvement, she acknowledged that several of them had seemed pretty frustrated at the end of the just-concluded budget preparation cycle. But when I suggested that she open up the process a bit by, for example, involving the board in an operational issues discussion early in the process, before any numbers had been put on paper, and that this would almost certainly turn her board into stronger owners of the ultimate budget, she really tightened up. "Look, it's my job to generate the budget and theirs to review it, and I'm not about to blur the lines!"

If you're a pretty board-savvy reader, you might ask yourself, "How could this CEO have climbed so high on the organizational ladder without learning the ins and outs of building a solid partnership with her board?" I can't be sure of the answer in this specific instance, but experience has taught me that there are two common reasons for such a narrow-minded, defensive approach to the governing game. In the first place, many CEOs get to the top without having mastered the nuts and bolts of the very complex business of governing, for a variety of reasons. Many have never worked directly with a board before, and so the governing arena is truly terra incognita. Others haven't managed to acquire much practical, tested guidance about boards and the board-CEO partnership through their reading and participation in educational programs. Keep in mind that even though boards have been around for nearly 400 years, only in the past decade or so have many books and educational programs on boards begun to appear.

For years I've been asking nonprofit and public board members, CEOs and senior executives participating in my workshops a question: "Who among you have taken a course in graduate school that paid detailed attention to the work of governing and building a solid board-CEO partnership?" The response? You might be surprised to know that the majority of the time, no hand is raised, and never more than three or four. Pretty ironic, isn't it, when you consider the authority and influence boards wield? Not only do they hire and fire the CEO, they have the power of the purse and can choose to support CEO priorities and strategies or not, and they can make the CEO's day-to-day life in the executive suite more or less comfortable. I can't think of a more important subject to teach in the field of nonprofit and public leadership and management, but even now you'll find much more attention paid to such technical functions as financial planning.

Secondly, you need to keep in mind that there's a lot of really bad advice out there, and believing everything you hear and read can be dangerous to your professional health. Allow me to share a real-life example. A couple of weeks ago the chief executive of a nonprofit serving adults and children with disabilities called me to discuss my facilitating a 1½-day strategic planning retreat for her board and executive team. She asked what I thought about devoting three or four hours of the retreat to developing her board's governing capacity, in addition to our visioning and issue identification work. I agreed that a governing session made the best of sense, and we got to talking about governing issues in her agency.

She kicked off our discussion by saying, "At the top of my list is getting my board downsized." "Oh really," I responded, "why is that?" It turns out that she'd recently attended a conference workshop at which the presenter, a board consultant, had observed that the "ideal" size of a nonprofit board was nine to fifteen members tops, and anyone with boards much larger than fifteen should seriously consider downsizing. "Well, Doug," she said, "by that standard, my twenty-five member board is an obvious candidate for downsizing." To make a long story short, after I pointed out that I had worked with any number of boards with more than twenty-five members that functioned as really high-impact governing bodies and that reducing her board's size would come at a steep cost in terms of diminished diversity, brainpower, access to resources, and political clout, we agreed that she should avoid the slippery slope of downsizing. We decided that it would make better sense to concentrate on clarifying her current board's role, updating its committee structure, and mapping out processes for more effective board involvement in such critical governing processes as strategic planning and performance monitoring.

This story is just another example of how much really bad advice—consisting of what I call fallacious little golden rules—is floating around in the governing arena. My counsel to my board development clients and other colleagues is caveat emptor—buyer beware! Be a cautious consumer of governing counsel; always be on guard, never take such advice at face value, and always, always, always think more than twice before acting. Take board downsizing, whose advocates more often than not, in my experience, base their fallacious small-is-better wisdom on a negative premise: "Boards are dangerous, always capable of micromanaging," they think, "and so we've got to keep the board small enough to maintain control and contain the threat." They seldom put it quite this baldly, but, believe me, that's where they're coming from. So caveat emptor should be your watch-word in the governing business.

Two other examples of fallacious—but oft proffered—advice best not taken come to mind. Some people have suggested that the board-CEO partnership can be actually managed by adopting policies that distinguish between the board's role and sphere of authority and the CEO's role and functions. This rule-making approach, sometimes called "policy governance," establishes clear boundaries, but misses the whole human dimension of board-CEO partnership building. Believe me, more than one CEO who has relied on rule making in developing his or her partnership with the board has ended up the victim of a soured relationship. Another dangerous but frequently recommended course of action is to make sure that you send finished staff work to your board, with all the t's crossed and i's dotted. Perhaps the most egregious example is the annual budget document, which many CEOs (see the example earlier in this chapter) believe should be complete when submitted to the board. Think about it for a minute. If the budget is complete when it hits the board, what is there for board members to do—other than serve as an admiring audience? I call this the thumbing-through approach to policy making. It's guaranteed to produce zero ownership or satisfaction among the thumbers.

## AN EMPOWERED BOARD

I opened this chapter by suggesting that really board-savvy CEOs are passionately committed to board empowerment, and they put their money where their mouth is by, first, not getting caught up in defensive routines aimed at protecting their turf from the board, and, second, by taking the lead in developing their board's governing capacity. What does an empowered board look like? Here's my definition, with which the great majority of board-savvy CEOs I've worked with would agree:

> An empowered board plays a proactive, creative role in making high-impact governing decisions and judgments—in close partnership with the CEO and senior executives—that answer three fundamental organizational questions:
>
>> 1. The Strategic Question: Where do we want our organization to head and what do we want it to become over the long run?
>>
>> 2. The Operational Question: What should our organization be now and in the near-term?
>>
>> 3. The Accountability Question: How is our organization performing—programmatically, financially, and administratively?

An empowered board also collaborates with the CEO and senior executives (often through board standing committees) in mapping out the processes for board member involvement in making these governing decisions and judgments, which tend to flow along three broad streams: strategic and operational planning; performance monitoring; and external/stakeholder relations.

## THE CHIEF BOARD CAPACITY BUILDER HAT

Since this is a book on the human (psychological/emotional) dimension of board-CEO partnership building, it wouldn't be appropriate to get into a lot of technical detail on the board capacity building (what is popularly known as board development) process. Instead, I'll briefly describe what the process entails and then take a look at the human concerns that you should take into account when you don the Chief Board Capacity Builder hat. So what is board development? In a nutshell, you can develop your board the same as you can develop any other human organization, in order to make it more effective at its core function—to govern—by:

- Clarifying your board's role: for example, by adopting a detailed board governing mission, setting out the board's major governing functions and responsibilities.

- Enriching your board's composition: for example, by adding seats for important stakeholder groups.

- Updating your board's governing structure: for example, by putting in place standing committees that correspond to your board's major streams of decisions and judgments (planning, monitoring, external relations).

- Mapping out processes for involving board members pro-actively and creatively in such major governing processes as strategic planning, budgeting, and performance monitoring.

- Strengthening your board's capacity to manage itself as a governing body: for example, by adopting board member performance targets and monitoring performance.

A board-savvy CEO serving as his or her organization's Chief Board Capacity Builder must:

- Be knowledgeable enough about developments in the rapidly changing field of nonprofit/public governance to

24

help the board make informed development decisions and to avoid the fallacious little golden rules that I discussed earlier in this chapter.

•Get board members interested in developing their board's governing capacity so that they are willing to participate in the development process and are open to change.

•Help the board put in place a capacity-building process that will not only come up with concrete initiatives to strengthen the board's role, structure, and processes, but will also build board member ownership of, and commitment to, the initiatives.

•Provide the executive support to make sure that the development process that is ultimately employed actually works.

## A WORD ABOUT BOARD DEVELOPMENT

Board-savvy CEOs who are dedicated to building a close, positive, and enduring partnership with their boards know that two approaches to board development that have often been used in the past would definitely be counter-productive: (1) the CEO's coming to the board with development recommendations (for example, "Here's the committee structure you should adopt, based on my serious study of the field."); and (2) hiring a consultant to study the organization's governing practices and to prepare an action report to the board recommending the steps that need to be taken. The problem with these traditional approaches isn't that they tend to produce irrational or technically deficient initiatives. It's serious attention to the human dimension that's lacking. These two bankrupt approaches, very simply, turn board members into an audience for recommendations that they played little if any part in shaping and consequently feel no ownership of or commitment to. The initiatives are, in effect, dead on arrival.

25

In my experience, board-savvy CEOs have gotten their boards to commit to—and strongly support—two basic approaches that, because they involve board members in shaping board development recommendations, have proved to be powerful board development vehicles, resulting in strong board ownership of initiatives that are ultimately implemented:

●**The Board Governance Retreat**
The whole board, along with the CEO and senior executives, spends a day or more in a retreat setting away from the office. With the help of a professional facilitator who is highly knowledgeable about nonprofit and public governance, participants familiarize themselves with the field, identify governing issues needing attention, and brainstorm possible initiatives (using breakout groups led by board members—a tried and true technique for breeding feelings of ownership). The facilitator, drawing on the work done at the retreat, prepares a report with concrete recommendations, presents it to an ad hoc implementation committee consisting of board members and the CEO. The implementation committee asks for revisions, and after reaching agreement on the content, presents the recommended board development initiatives to the full board.

●**The Governance Task Force**
The board chair appoints a governance task force consisting of board members and the CEO. The task force retains the services of a knowledgeable governance consultant and, over the course of four to six meetings, works with the consultant in coming up with recommended board development initiatives. The task force members, with the consultant in a backup role, present the recommendations to the full board.

Both of these approaches have a high success rate because of the intensive involvement of board members in shaping recommendations, which fosters feelings of ownership. Note that in both cases board members present the recommendations to the full board, further strengthening board ownership and commitment since board members tend to be more receptive to suggestions from their peers than from outsiders such as consultants.

# KEY #2:
# MAKE YOUR BOARD CHAIR
# A CLOSE ALLY

A STAKEHOLDER IS A PERSON, group, or organizational entity with which it makes sense for you to maintain a relationship of some kind because of the stakes involved. Obviously, the higher the stakes, the more attention you'd want to pay to a particular stakeholder relationship. Board-savvy CEOs put their board at the top of the list of critical stakeholders, professionally speaking, and coming in a close second would be the board chair (or president in the case of school boards and many associations). Your board chair is always a force to be reckoned with, for four very important reasons:

1. Your board chair is, in effect, the chief executive of your board, responsible in this capacity for leading board meeting deliberations, heading the executive (now often known as governance or board operations) committee, appointing the chairs and members of the board's standing committees and ad hoc bodies, and more.

2. Your board chair is normally seen as a major—and often the primary—ambassador from your nonprofit or public organization to the wider world, including representing your organization to the media and speaking on behalf of your organization in important external forums.

3. Your board chair, because he or she is typically elected by the board or an association's membership, has significant influence and clout; when he or she speaks, people listen.

4. And your board chair is commonly seen as the board's day-to-day liaison between the CEO and the board.

## WHAT'S YOUR STRATEGY?

In light of the high stakes involved, any board-savvy CEO will see the need to pay close attention to his or her relationship with the board chair. The challenge is to come up with a detailed strategy for building and maintaining a working relationship that is productive and mutually satisfying. Over the years I've seen a number of un-savvy CEOs employ two notoriously ineffective strategies that you are well-advised to avoid like the plague. One is what I call the Marshmallow Strategy. CEOs in this camp—a weak-kneed lot if there ever was one—essentially see their role as passively adapting to whatever chair happens to come along, basically accepting the chairs' views on the division of labor and helping them achieve whatever goals they've set for themselves. At best, this wimpy strategy doesn't result in any significant harm because the board chair doesn't feel competitive with the CEO and isn't interested in imposing particular programmatic priorities or initiatives on the organization.

However, when a board chair arrives on the scene who sees himself or herself in competition with the CEO—indeed, often seeing the role as a kind of "co-CEOship"—or who is a zealous advocate of a particular programmatic course of action (which might very well be technically ill-conceived, financially risky, or in conflict with the stated core values of the organization), then you've got a real problem on your hands. I've seen this kind of situation develop most often in associations, especially where the board chair is given the title "president," and the CEO a very un-CEO-like title, such as "executive vice president" or "chief staff executive." Such unfortunate titling fosters misunderstanding and invites conflict.

The other high-risk approach, which I call the Keep in Your Place Strategy, is at the other end of the spectrum. This arms-length and defensive approach is aimed at preventing whatever board chair happens to come along from meddling in the CEO's business and from launching any personal initiatives that might

30

do harm. In many ways this more calcium-laden approach is preferable to the Marshmallow Strategy, but because it doesn't involve creative thinking about the board chair role or the chair-CEO relationship, it tends to create a dangerous vacuum: an underemployed board chair who is typically an ambitious, aggressive Type A becomes ever more frustrated, perhaps even angry, and eventually the CEO's adversary.

The really board-savvy CEOs I've seen over the years eschew both of these non-productive approaches and opt instead for what I call the Governing Ally Strategy. Allow me to paraphrase how one of the savviest CEOs I've worked with recently described this strategy:

> I really want my board chair to be in my corner—a close partner whom I can count on to be my advocate and champion with the board on issues close to my heart. I see the two of us as a real leadership team, with both of us playing a significant leadership role. One of my most important CEO responsibilities is to think creatively about my chair's leadership role and potential accomplishments and to map out a strategy for supporting my chair in playing this role successfully. Sure, there's always potential for conflict, but the more I strategize about our partnership, and devote time and attention to keeping it healthy, the less likely we'll end up at loggerheads.

Here are five steps that CEOs who adhere to the Governing Ally Strategy have taken to build a really solid partnership with their board chairs; I'll describe each in some detail:

1. Get acquainted—in-depth—with your board chair.

2. Reach detailed agreement on the basic division of labor between the two of you, paying special attention to your chair's role as CEO of the board and his or her involvement in external relations.

3. Make sure that your chair succeeds in the board CEO role.

4. Help your chair achieve his or her professional objectives.

5. And take advantage of every opportunity to turn your chair into a real owner, rather than just a figurehead or bystander.

## GETTING TO KNOW YOUR BOARD CHAIR

The better you know your board chair the more successful you're likely to be in building and maintaining a positive and productive partnership. The really board-savvy superintendent of a large, rapidly growing school district in the southwestern United States has had notable success in building effective partnerships with her school board presidents over the years. (Although their official title is board "president," I'll use the more standard title "chair" from this point on.) She makes a point of spending several hours with every new chair early in his or her tenure—usually over several breakfast and lunch meetings—becoming thoroughly acquainted with her new colleague at the top. One major benefit of this early, very intensive interaction is personal bonding with her new chair. Knowing that friendship is a powerful lubricant, this board-savvy superintendent really does aim to develop a relationship with every one of her board chairs that is more than strictly business focused, without ever threatening professionalism.

Beyond bonding, early personal interaction has served this board-savvy superintendent well in breaking down erroneous impressions that her new board chair might bring to the new relationship. For example, one of her new chairs, who was newly elected to the board and had been publicly and loudly critical of several of the superintendent's decisions over the past year, had perceived the superintendent as an aloof administrator preoccupied with management system development at the expense of education. But when he got to know the superintendent better, he learned that she was passionate about education and deeply committed to student success, both in the classroom and later in life. Don't think for a minute that these corrected impressions didn't contribute to what became a productive board chair-superintendent working partnership.

What this board-savvy superintendent wants to know early in her relationships with her various board chairs relates to leadership style, personal professional interests and objectives, and ego needs. Her mission, as she explained to me over the course of a fascinating couple of lunches—and as I observed in action over the year I worked with her—was to put this detailed knowledge to work in cementing a mutually beneficial working relationship with her board chair. As her district's CEO she believes (as I do) that she is responsible, within reason, for adapting to her president's leadership style, for helping her president pursue her professional interests and objectives, and for helping her president find ego satisfaction in carrying out her leadership role—all without violating canons of professional conduct or good taste. Let's look at some real-life examples of this partnership-building philosophy in action.

## REGARDING LEADERSHIP STYLE

Her various board chairs over the years sometimes varied dramatically in the ways they learned and applied knowledge in arriving at conclusions and making decisions. For example, one of her brightest and most ambitious chairs wasn't a reader, and it wouldn't have been helpful to supply him with a written briefing exploring the pros and cons of a complex issue, such as re-drawing school district boundaries. So, although our board-savvy superintendent was highly comfortable with written communication, and a superb writer to boot, she adapted by making sure she and this particular chair spent ample face-to-face time working through issues. It proved to be a sound strategy for both educating him and getting his support on important issues, and, by the way, it also earned his appreciation. Of course, other chairs over the years have demanded—and received—beautifully crafted memoranda setting out options and offering recommendations. In her mind, her board chair is always a customer to be satisfied, and adapting to differing learning and decision-making styles is a pretty inexpensive way of turning chairs into satisfied customers.

As this board-savvy superintendent is keenly aware, her board chair's leadership style also relates to his or her public role. Over the years, she's encountered board chairs who want to play a visible and assertive role in getting the school board to make critical decisions, and who see themselves—at least for the truly high-stakes issues—as change champions for the superintendent. When this is the case, our board-savvy superintendent has always gone out of her way to take advantage of this style, always cautioning her chair, of course, not to come across too strongly and preempt standing committees or alienate other board members. By contrast, when she's working with a school board chair who doesn't relish an up-front role but, instead, is more comfortable facilitating deliberations and working behind the scenes on consensus building, she adapts to this very different style. She never, ever tries to fit the proverbial square peg in the round hole!

## INTERESTS, OBJECTIVES AND EGO NEEDS

Our board-savvy superintendent also pays close attention to learning about her board chairs' passionate professional interests, what they really want to achieve as board chairs, the imprint they want to leave, and what matters to them ego-wise. Her mission is, within reason, to provide her chairs with opportunities for in-depth involvement in areas that especially interest them (for example, special education; performing and fine arts programming), to help her chairs to achieve their major professional objectives (for example, becoming a more accomplished public speaker; to become active in the state school boards association); and to find ego satisfaction where it matters (for example, the need to be seen as an educational statesperson; the need for media attention). Since I'll be discussing this dimension in more detail below, suffice it to say at this point that our board-savvy superintendent is keenly aware of the levers that need to be pulled to cement her relationship with her board chairs, and she pulls them.

## CHAIR-CEO DIVISION OF LABOR

The president and CEO of a chamber of commerce in a mid-size midwestern city learned after a few years in the top spot that many, if not most, new chamber board chairs that are elected to work with him will bring only a vague understanding of the chair's role to the partnership, and every now and then a new chair will arrive who is just plain wrongheaded about the role. For example, he's had new chairs who see themselves as essentially in a ceremonial role with no responsibility for the board's governing decisions and judgments, and he's had chairs who see themselves as co-CEOs. This board-savvy chamber CEO makes it a point very early in the relationship with his new board chair to sit him or her down for a detailed, very explicit discussion of the basic division of labor between the two and the fundamental ground rules. He wants his board chair to understand and agree that:

•The board chair is essentially the "CEO" of the board, responsible for leading its governing deliberations.

•The CEO is responsible for all internal operations of the chamber.

•The external relations turf is a shared chair-CEO responsibility, requiring a carefully negotiated division of labor and considerable collaboration.

Certain rules of the game will help to ensure a sound working relationship, including, among others, that:

- Only the board as a whole can give direction to the CEO, never the board chair alone.

- The whole board, or a designated committee of the board, is responsible for evaluating CEO performance, never the board chair alone.

- The board chair never gives direction to staff under the CEO.

- Neither the board chair nor the CEO ever take public positions on major issues without the formal concurrence of the full board.

The chamber CEO we're discussing, along with many other board-savvy CEOs, in my experience, have learned that it is very useful to have this fundamental division of labor and set of interaction guidelines formally adopted by the whole board and incorporated into a board operating manual of some kind. Otherwise, there will be a clear and present danger that a wrongheaded but very strong-spoken and persuasive board chair can blur the lines and cause real trauma. And I've come across many cases where an organization's bylaws need to be amended because they sow confusion and undermine the chair-CEO relationship. For example, I've worked with national associations whose bylaws actually call the board chair the "president" and the CEO a lame title like "executive vice president" or "chief staff executive." These strange titles aren't recognized in the wider world as CEO titles, so they can contribute to serious role confusion and needless dysfunction. Even worse, I recently came across a set of bylaws that defined the board chair as the "chief executive officer" and the CEO (called the "executive director" in this instance) as the "chief administrative officer."

I've seen board chair-CEO relationships come to grief in the external relations area because the division of labor remains vague. The highly successful, board-savvy chamber executive I've been discussing has put together the following strategy, which has proved very effective in practice:

•He discusses in detail early in his board chair's tenure what facets of the external relations agenda his chair is most interested in: Being booked to speak on behalf of the chamber in such forums as the monthly Rotary luncheon meeting? Participating in important meetings with critical stakeholders, such as the board of education or community college president? Being involved with the media, for example, being interviewed by newspaper reporters or participating in radio or TV public affairs panels? Presenting workshops at the annual state chamber association meeting or at national meetings?

•He reaches agreement with his board chair on a schedule of external relations engagements that they will handle separately or together (for example, submitting a proposal to present a workshop at the next annual conference of the American Chamber of Commerce Executives).

•He makes sure that his chair is provided with the support he or she needs to succeed in representing the chamber (for example, an attractive set of PowerPoint slides for the Rotary luncheon meeting; or a briefing paper before a press interview).

•And he is always on the lookout for new opportunities for his chair to represent the chamber in the external world (for example, a call comes from the county executive's office asking the chamber to designate someone to represent it on the new countywide economic development commission being put together). One of the CEO's little golden rules is that he never just accepts an invitation for himself without thinking about the board chair first.

Later in this book I'll be talking about the whole board's involvement in the external relations arena, under the leadership of a board external relations committee. So you need to keep in mind that the board chair and CEO don't have exclusive ownership of this agenda and that participation in external relations is one of the powerful vehicles for generating feelings of ownership and ego satisfaction among all board members.

## ENSURING YOUR CHAIR'S SUCCESS IN LEADING THE BOARD

The board-savvy CEO of a large, rapidly growing retirement community in New England, offering the full spectrum of services from assisted living apartments to a skilled nursing facility, makes a point of preparing her board chair for board meetings, knowing that letting him sink or swim in leading board deliberations would be a high-risk course of action. Her strategy includes:

•Running over the tentative agenda of the upcoming board meeting with the chair before discussing it with the board operations committee, where it is finalized.

•Making sure her board chair thoroughly understands any complex agenda items that will be introduced at the board meeting so that he or she can be an effective facilitator of discussion.

•And also drafting a regular board chair's report, describing the chair's external activities on behalf of the agency since the last board meeting.

Making her board chair look in command at every board meeting has proved to be a critical ingredient in the glue cementing the chair-CEO partnership.

## HELPING YOUR CHAIR ACHIEVE
## PROFESSIONAL OBJECTIVES

The board-savvy general manager of a public transportation authority in a large, urban county in the Northeast makes a point of knowing what his board chair wants to achieve professionally from his unpaid service as the board's leader, and he goes out of his way to help his chair achieve these objectives, knowing that such nonmonetary compensation is a powerful relationship builder. For example, one of his chairs had higher political aspirations, but wasn't a very effective performer at the lectern in large public meetings. This board chair, recognizing that his inadequacies as a public speaker would be a serious barrier to his political success, shared his need for help with the CEO, who made a real effort to help his chair become a capable, if not outstanding, speaker by making sure he was booked to speak regularly (beginning with smaller, safer venues), supplying him with presentation aids such as PowerPoint slides and handouts, and actually making sure he had opportunities to rehearse and receive constructive feedback.

Another of this transportation CEO's board chairs—an entrepreneur who had built a highly profitable computer services business—shared his keen interest in countywide economic development, not only because he was passionately interested in the county's economic and social well-being, but also because significant population and job loss over the past couple of decades threatened the bottom line of his own company. So the CEO did some behind-the-scenes lobbying to secure his chair's appointment to the county workforce development board, and when the county administrator invited the CEO to serve on the newly formed countywide economic development commission, the CEO put forward his chair's name instead. Now, this board-savvy CEO well knew that it wasn't enough merely to get his chair appointed to these two economic development bodies. He had to provide a minimum level of support to help his chair flourish in these roles. One very practical step he took in this regard was to assign a couple of his senior executives to provide the chair with expert analysis and counsel on particular issues coming before these economic development bodies, as the chair requested. Yes, there was some slight potential for abuse of staff time, but in practice it didn't occur.

## TURNING YOUR BOARD CHAIR INTO AN OWNER

In the next chapter I describe some practical steps that board-savvy CEOs can take to turn all of their board members into owners, rather than just treating them as a passive-reactive audience. However, every highly successful CEO I've worked with over the past twenty-five years has treated his or her board chair as the preeminent owner on the board. In this regard, I've seen two strategies work very effectively:

1. They make sure that their chair is actively involved in guiding and coordinating the work of the board, primarily through heading a "governance" or "board operations" committee. Consisting of the other board committee chairs and the CEO, this standing committee of the board is responsible, among other things, for developing the board agenda, setting board member performance targets, monitoring board member performance, evaluating the whole board's performance as a governing body, and establishing board improvement objectives.

2. And they also make sure that their board chair is a leading player in any concentrated board development initiatives that are launched to take a thoroughgoing look at the board's role, structure, and processes. At the very least, if an ad hoc board committee is put together to assess the board's performance as a governing body and to come up with concrete recommendations for strengthening the board's role, structure, and processes, the board-savvy CEO makes sure

that the detailed charge to the ad hoc committee comes from the board chair and that the board chair is regularly briefed on progress. Most often, the board-savvy CEO goes beyond that minimal role, convincing the board chair to head the ad hoc committee and to be involved in detail in its deliberations from beginning to end.

# KEY #3:
# TURN YOUR BOARD MEMBERS INTO STRONG OWNERS

A COUPLE OF YEARS AGO, the executive director of a nonprofit providing services to children with mental disabilities told me about a serious error of judgment during his first eighteen months on the job a little over a decade ago. "It was immediately obvious to me," he told me over lunch, "that one of the most pressing CEO challenges I'd have to address sooner rather than later was the need for an updated strategic plan for the agency." Just continuing along the business-as-usual road, he pointed out, would lead to organizational decline, for which he'd ultimately be held accountable, in light of the rapidly changing and challenging environment—including declining state funding and growing competition. "My new board really had to make some critical growth-oriented strategic investments, above and beyond our programs and services already in place— and soon—but to do so rationally required an updated, detailed vision for the future and a firm handle on the strategic growth opportunities and the challenges meriting attention." So he had to get going on the strategic planning front, and that's what he did.

In a special meeting, this new CEO's executive committee authorized him to send a request for proposals to eight consulting firms with solid nonprofit experience and agreed to an adequate, if not handsome, budget to fund the effort and to a target date four months hence for submission of the finished strategic plan to the board. Not even three weeks later a firm was under contract, and the strategic planning show was on the road. The consulting team reviewed a mountain of documentation, interviewed some thirty-five board members and staff, and met several times with the staff steering committee that the CEO had put together to guide the planning effort to review the various sections of the strategic plan as they were drafted (for example, the summary of trends and conditions; the description of strategic issues facing the agency; the updated vision statement). The CEO briefed the board on progress at its regular business meetings while the plan was being developed, but that was the extent of board involvement. The board, by the way, didn't have a planning committee, which would have been a natural candidate for more detailed involvement.

The finished strategic plan that was presented to the board was a beautifully crafted document, and the consulting team did an impressive job of presenting it and answering questions. The CEO told me over lunch that he had tears in his eyes when the board unanimously passed a resolution adopting the strategic plan after only ninety minutes of discussion. Armed with firm agreement at the top on strategic directions, the CEO could move forward aggressively on the detailed planning front, getting concrete initiatives launched to diversify programming and get new revenue streams flowing. And everyone worked happily ever after, right? If you've spent much time working with boards, you know that wasn't the case. Over the next several months, the strategic initiatives that were submitted to the board for review and approval were debated endlessly, and it was clear that the deliberations weren't being guided by the vision statement that had been adopted along with the other sections of the strategic plan. In fact, board members, as they were discussing particular initiatives, often observed that it would be helpful to have a better sense of "where we're headed over the long run" before making any final decisions, as if they hadn't reviewed and approved the vision statement only a few months earlier.

So this beautifully crafted, really quite rational, handsomely bound plan didn't have much impact in the short run in terms of this children's services agency investing in concrete growth and diversification initiatives, and not much more than a year after it had been adopted, it was sitting on the shelf, gathering dust and never consulted. Why this sad ending? Not because the plan was technically deficient, to be sure, but because the process of producing the plan treated board members as an audience for finished consultant work, rather than turning them into real owners.

## OWNERSHIP: A POWERFUL FORCE

The board-savviest CEOs I've worked with over the past two decades pay close attention to transforming their board members into strong owners of their governing work: the governing decisions and judgments they make and the critical governing products they generate (for example, an updated vision statement or the annual budget). Experience has taught them that board members who feel like owners make more reliable partners who can be depended on not to fade away when the going gets tough. When a board truly owns a governing product such as an updated vision statement, that board is firmly committed to that vision statement, and the odds that it will end up gathering dust on the proverbial shelf, exerting little if any influence, are slim. Ownership and commitment are natural partners.

So how can you turn your board members into real owners of their governing work and products? In my experience, there's only one reliable way: you've got to ensure that your board members are systematically and formally involved in:

•Mapping out the processes (for example, strategic planning; budgeting; performance monitoring) for involving board members in making the decisions and judgments that constitute their governing work. What board work sessions, for example, will be held as the annual budget document is being developed? What will board members do in these sessions? How long will this last? Who will run them?

•Ensuring that these governing processes involve board members proactively and substantively in shaping the major governing products (such as a values statement or set of strategic goals). Board member involvement is proactive when it occurs early enough in a process such as strategic planning to have significant influence in shaping outcomes, rather than board members merely serving as an audience for an essentially finished strategic plan late in the planning process. By "substantive," I mean that the involvement makes full use of board members' intelligence, experience, expertise, knowledge, and diverse perspectives.

## FIVE CRITICAL STEPS

Board-savvy CEOs know that there are five critical steps they can take to turn their board members into owners of their governing work:

1. Wear the Chief Process Designer hat, taking the lead in designing processes for involving board members in ways that generate feelings of ownership.

2. Put in place a modern board standing committee structure that corresponds to the actual flows of governing decisions and judgments (board self-management, planning, monitoring, external relations).

3. Use these contemporary standing committees as vehicles both for detailed board member involvement in governing and for continuously updating the processes for board member involvement.

4. Put in place committee operating guidelines that promote board member ownership.

5. And take steps to ensure that committee chairs visibly succeed in leading their committees.

46

## PROCESS DESIGN HAT

As I've traveled around the country the past few years, working with nonprofit and public boards and CEOs, I've seen a new model of CEO leadership emerge. It's not that the old-time model has disappeared, but it's definitely been significantly expanded. There's still a need for a visionary leader who inspires the troops and builds relationships with critical external stakeholders, who stops the buck at his or her desk, who is the master of such critical executive functions as strategic and financial planning, and who takes accountability for whatever happens on his or her watch. But in recent years a critical new responsibility has been added to this CEO mix: Chief Process Designer.

Putting on the Chief Process Designer hat is the critical first step you must take as CEO in building your board members' ownership of their governing work, for two primary reasons. First, board members become owners of their governing work through participation in governing processes such as strategic planning and performance monitoring—processes that are explicitly designed to foster such ownership. Second, it makes the best of sense for the CEO to take the lead in designing process; it's not realistic to expect the part-time volunteers who populate boards to keep up with developments in fields such as strategic planning or to put in the time necessary to map out the detailed steps involved in coming up with an updated strategic plan. Of course, board members must be involved in process design—primarily, as I discuss below, through board standing committees—but they can't realistically be the lead designer.

Wearing the Chief Process Designer hat means you've got to invest significant time in understanding the state of the art in major governing areas; otherwise, you might recommend that your board members invest precious time and energy in an outmoded approach that fails to meet expectations, not only disappointing and dispiriting your board members, but also damaging your credibility as CEO. Take that gold standard for board involvement: strategic planning. Old-time comprehensive long-range planning for arbitrary and meaningless periods such as five years is now dead as a doornail, for the simple reason that, for all the trees that have been sacrificed and hours and dollars spent producing monster five-year plans, virtually no significant strategic change has been generated. To be blunt, five-year planning is a dud as a tool for leading strategic change in a changing, challenging world. At the very best, it's a great tool for describing what an organization is already doing and hence can be an effective educational and external relations tool. But it tends to be a highly dangerous planning tool, lulling organizations into a sense of false security: "Now that we've mapped our goals and programs out five years into the future, we can relax a bit, knowing that we've got things pretty well under control." Fatal last words if there ever were ones!

Wearing the Chief Process Designer hat also means that you spend lots of time mapping out the steps involved in generating key governing products such as a vision statement, a set of core values, or an annual budget and giving serious thought to the kinds of steps that are likely to prove most effective at building board member ownership. As you well know, there is seldom only one path you can follow on the way to a desired end (for example, adopting the annual budget), and so it's well worth your time to play around with different approaches to involving board members, with an eye not only to maximizing board member time but also to maximizing feelings of ownership. The dangerous alternative to immersing yourself in the details of process design is to take the lead of a highly vocal board member who's passionate about a "pet" approach that hasn't been tested in your kind of nonprofit or of a consultant with a vested interest in selling you his boilerplate package.

## WELL-DESIGNED STANDING COMMITTEES

Board-savvy CEOs know that well-designed board standing committees are the single most powerful tool for transforming board members into real owners of their governing work, and thereby into solid partners that you can depend on through thick and thin. What do I mean by well-designed? My first Governance Edge book, *Meeting the Governing Challenge*, describes a model board committee structure in detail, so I'll only point out here that a well-designed committee needs to correspond to one of the major streams of governing judgments and decisions that your board regularly makes when it governs. Following this design criterion, your board needs a structure consisting of:

•A governance or board operations committee to co-ordinate the board's governing activities, to set board performance targets and monitor board performance, and to handle the development of board member governing knowledge and skills.

•A planning committee to design and coordinate the board's involvement in the strategic and operational planning process, including development of the annual budget document.

•A performance oversight and monitoring committee to design and review programmatic and financial performance reports, identifying significant performance problems.

•And an external relations committee to design and co-ordinate board member involvement in your nonprofit's image-building and public relations activities.

Now, if your board's structure corresponds to your board's governing work, these well-designed standing committees can build board member ownership in three major ways:

1. Well-designed standing committees can serve as continuous governing improvement vehicles. Committee members

can work closely with the CEO and senior executives in reaching agreement on the detailed processes for involving board members in their respective areas, touching up these processes year after year to produce stronger outcomes and further strengthen board member ownership of the outcomes. You can easily see that your board as a whole would be an unwieldy vehicle for accomplishing such detailed process design work.

2. The in-depth involvement of committee members in their respective functional areas builds committee members' governing knowledge and expertise—a powerful means of fostering feelings of ownership among board members. Take, for example, your performance oversight and monitoring committee's detailed review of the quarterly financial report comparing actual to budgeted expenditures by major cost center, for the quarter and year-to-date. The opportunity to dig into the details, to ask probing questions, to spend time exploring operational shortfalls, and the like, breeds understanding and hence ownership. By contrast, board members' serving merely as an audience for the financial report in a regular business meeting has zero ownership-building potential.

3. Your committee chairs, by virtue of their highly visible positions as leaders of well-designed standing committees, very quickly become strong owners of the board's governing work and, when a really board-savvy CEO plays his or her cards right, can become preeminent CEO partners, second only to the board chair.

## SOME CRITICAL COMMITTEE GUIDELINES

Many nonprofit and public boards I've worked with over the years have formally adopted guidelines to govern their standing committees, in order to ensure that they function effectively.

Three guidelines have proved, in my experience, to be very useful in fostering board member ownership:

1. Make sure that every board member is assigned to a standing committee, with no exceptions, and that committee attendance and participation are formally identified board member performance targets.

2. Require that the only way an item—whether for information or action—can get on the board business meeting agenda is through the appropriate standing committee.

3. And also require that all reports at regular board business meetings be presented by committee chairs and members and never by staff (except as invited to comment as part of the committee's report).

## TURNING COMMITTEE CHAIRS INTO SUPER-OWNERS AND CEO PARTNERS

In my experience, board standing committee chairs can become super-owners and CEO partners, second in importance only to the board chair. However, a "bump on the log" chair whose leadership role is obviously ceremonial and who participates as an equal with other committee members won't realize his or her potential as either owner or partner. What's required is strong, consistent executive support to ensure that your committee chairs visibly succeed in leading committee deliberations. In this regard, many nonprofit and public CEOs appoint a member of their executive/senior management team to serve as the Chief Staff Liaison to each of the standing committees, in this capacity:

•Working closely with their committee chair in developing committee agenda.

•Making sure their committee chairs thoroughly understand—and can lead discussion on—complex agenda items.

•Drafting their committee chair's report to the board.

•And making their chair's reports at board meetings more effective by, for example, developing PowerPoint slides that employ creative graphics.

## A CLOSER LOOK AT THE COMMITTEE DESIGN PROCESS

I'll close this chapter on turning your board members into owners of their governing work by looking at two examples of steps that real-life board standing committees have designed into their processes for board member involvement in their respective governing areas, working in close partnership with the CEO and senior executives.

### A BOARD OPERATIONS COMMITTEE

The Board Operations Committee of a school board developed a set of board member governing performance targets and interaction guidelines that, after considerable discussion, were adopted by the full board and incorporated into the board's official policy manual. To take some examples, board members were expected to: attend and participate actively in the standing committees to which the board president assigned them; come prepared for committee and full board meetings, having thoroughly reviewed the packets of information sent to them in advance; speak on behalf of the school district in public forums, as specified by the board's community relations committee, at least once a quarter; not to bring hidden agendas to committee and board meetings; not to publicly criticize decisions made by a board majority. Of course, board members couldn't be legally required to follow these guidelines, and some board members expressed skepticism that they would have any appreciable impact on the board's performance as a governing body. However, in the years since the first set of performance targets were adopted (they've been fine-tuned from year-to-year), it is obvious, judging from board member testimonials, that just having a set of formal performance targets that they had developed themselves, irrespective of their content, has boosted the board's self-esteem (signaling to the wider world that they are not an ordinary governing body), and, as a consequence, strengthened board member ownership of the board and its governing processes.

## A PLANNING AND DEVELOPMENT COMMITTEE

The Planning and Development Committee of a national association designed a 1½-day strategic work session into its annual planning cycle as a means of involving board members creatively and proactively in the strategic direction-setting process and thereby building their ownership of the directions ultimately coming out of the process. Features of the strategic work session design were explicitly intended to strengthen board member ownership, including:

•The use of nine breakout groups led by board members to generate content through a brainstorming methodology, for example: a values and vision statement; conditions and trends pertinent to the association's mission; an assessment of the association's strengths and weaknesses in key areas, such as delivering educational services to members; the identification of strategic issues appearing to deserve serious attention in the near term.

•Avoidance of any formal decision making in the work session, so that participants could freely share their ideas and questions without worrying about making bad decisions.

•Detailed agreement on the process for following through on the session, including the Planning and Development Committee's analysis of the breakout group reports and formulation of follow-through actions, which would be presented to the full board in a special work session.

# KEY #4:
# MAKE YOUR BOARD'S WORK MORE INTERESTING AND ENJOYABLE

IN THE WORLD OF NONPROFIT and public leadership, what could possibly be more interesting and exciting than being involved in making the high-stakes decisions and judgments that constitute the work of governing? Rising above technical and operational details, board members lead a privileged organizational life, focusing on the real "biggies": values, vision, strategic issues, annual performance targets, resource allocation, assessments of performance, and more. If there's a downside, it's that governing work, no matter how interesting and even exciting, can't ever be a piece of cake. The work is by its very nature complex and demanding; it's always hard to do well and can at times be quite painful. The pain can be excruciating when dealing with inherently negative issues such as determining what programs to trim by how much in response to a revenue shortfall; selecting the bus routes to eliminate because of falling ridership; or deciding which school buildings to close because of dramatic demographic change in the community. But boring or uninteresting? Is that possible?

Well, sad to say, many boards, in my experience, often find themselves engaged in work that is boring and needlessly painful. For example, I once worked with an international association board whose meetings lasted for two whole days, and virtually all of that time was spent listening to incredibly detailed technical reports from a variety of advisory committees that for the most part called for no high-level board decision making. Talk about being buried in operational minutiae! My interviews with a dozen or so board members in preparation for a governance work session I was to facilitate indicated that board members didn't find their governing work particularly exciting, or even very interesting. And I worked with a public transportation board whose members waded through incredibly detailed financial reports in preparation for board meetings that were so complex that only a couple of board members had a firm grasp of the organization's financial situation. Financial understanding came at a price in terms of time and effort that most board members were reluctant to pay.

Experience has taught me that these two examples aren't the exceptions that prove the rule. Even though board members who find their governing work interesting and enjoyable tend to be better CEO partners, in practice maintaining board member interest and enjoyment is no small challenge for CEOs. Over the years I've interviewed thousands of board members in preparation for retreats that I've been retained to facilitate, and one of the questions I always ask is: "What's it like serving on the board—how does it feel?" No one in all this time has ever responded by saying anything close to "exciting" or "really enjoyable." "Pretty interesting" and "challenging" are as good as it gets. The great majority of board members I've interviewed have made a point of telling me that they find satisfaction in "making a difference" and highly value their association with their colleagues on the board. But whenever I've asked someone whether the thought of an upcoming board meeting makes the hair on the back of his or her neck stand up, the response is invariably a chuckle.

## PUTTING ON THE CHIEF THEATRICAL PRODUCER HAT

The board-savviest CEOs I've come across over the years know that board members who find their governing work interesting and enjoyable—and not needlessly painful—tend to make better CEO partners, and they accordingly keep another hat in their executive wardrobe, alongside their Chief Board Developer and Chief Process Designer hats: Chief Theatrical Producer. Wearing this hat, board-savvy CEOs pay close attention to practical ways to make their board's governing work more enjoyable and interesting and to minimize the pain of governing. Fostering board member interest and enjoyment isn't an end in itself to these board-savvy CEOs, but one of the important ways to keep the board-CEO partnership close, productive, and positive. Wearing the Chief Theatrical Producer hat, these CEOs have:

- Made sure that board members aren't trapped by out-moded governing structure.

- Used various means to raise board members' sights above the trench of day-to-day governing work.

- Upgraded reporting to the board.

- Spiced-up regular board meetings.

- Involved board members as ambassadors.

- And strengthened board members' personal interaction.

## AVOIDING THE TRAP OF OUTMODED STRUCTURE

Earlier in this chapter I talked about an association board whose meetings ran for two days and were filled with detailed technical and operational matters coming from several technical advisory committees. This is a classic case of being trapped by structure, but escape is possible:

- In the first place, this association board needed to put in place a structure of board governing committees that correspond to the streams of governing judgments and decisions that high-impact boards make (planning; performance monitoring; external relations). With the right structure in place—and the requirement that the governing committees be the only conduit to the full board meeting—the detailed technical and operational matters being forwarded from non-governing advisory committees could be screened out, leaving the governing wheat and eliminating the non-governing chaff.

•In the second place, a two-day board meeting makes no sense at all and is undoubtedly a vestige of a long-gone past, when association volunteers serving on the board were expected to manage the association's affairs, rather than rising above the details and actually making governing decisions and judgments. I've never encountered a board with a structure of real governing committees whose regular business meetings needed to last longer than a half-day, and the overwhelming majority of boards I've worked with over the past quarter century have accomplished their work in meetings lasting no more than two hours.

Keep in mind that, following the first-things-first rule, you've got to deal with serious structural flaws before moving on to other strategies for making your board members' governing work more interesting and enjoyable. No matter how hard you try, you're not likely to make much progress with a poorly designed structure in place.

## RAISING BOARD MEMBERS' SIGHTS

Experience has taught me that the great majority of nonprofit and public board members bring to their governing work both a sincere desire to make a real difference and a tremendous capacity for hard work. However, a few years of laboring in the governing trenches, even when the board is involved in making truly high-impact decisions and judgments, can erode your board members' sense of mission and drain much of their enthusiasm and energy. Having read thousands of pages of board minutes over the past two decades, I know that the regular, month-by-month or quarter-by-quarter work of governing can be quite deadly. One of the most important ways you can combat governing fatigue and reenergize your board members, giving them a new lease on their governing life, is to raise their sights above the governing trenches. I've seen three approaches work quite well in this regard:

1.  Involve your board members intensively at the open end of the "strategic funnel" (moving from a wide opening through an ever-narrowing "spout" that symbolizes the application of disciplined decision-making and implementation activities).

2.  Expose them to education and training opportunities.

3.  Share experiences from your travels in the CEO fast lane.

Strategic decision making is the gold standard for board participation in the affairs of your organization, as I've observed before, not only because of the high stakes involved in dealing with strategic issues, but also because board members are uniquely qualified to contribute at the open end of the strategic funnel—where your organization's vision and values are revisited, environmental conditions and trends are reviewed, the strategic issues facing your organization are identified, and possible change initiatives to deal with the issues are brainstormed. No other process is so effective, in my experience, at raising your board members' sights above the governing trenches.

An annual strategic work session or retreat, kicking off your organization's annual planning process, is a sure-fire way to involve your board productively at the open end of the strategic funnel, and you can design the session so that it not only raises your board members' sights, but also provides them with a thoroughly enjoyable experience. For example, retreat planners at a school district I recently worked with made sure that participants were fully engaged by using several breakout groups that employed a brainstorming methodology and enriched the session by inviting a number of the district's important stakeholders to participate, including the superintendent of a neighboring district and local elected officials.

You can also raise your board members' sights by calling their attention to developments in their mother field (for example, association leadership and management for a state or national association) and even in the extended family (public/nonprofit leadership). I'm now working with a national association board that accomplishes this through a formal board member education and training program planned and coordinated by the board's governance committee. The program consists of board member participation in the annual meeting of the American Society of Association Executives on a rotating basis; speakers on pertinent topics at board meetings; and a board lending library that circulates articles and books among board members dealing with issues in the association's industry and developments in the field of association governance.

And board-savvy CEOs know that most, if not all, of their board members are likely to be an avid audience for briefings on the nonroutine CEO activities that they engage in, such as service on state or local boards, meetings with leaders in the field or community, speaking engagements, and the like. Making an effort to fill your board members in on the more interesting and exciting aspects of your CEO work, in person and via fax and e-mail briefings, is a simple, inexpensive way to spice up their governing life.

## UPGRADING REPORTING TO THE BOARD

Yes, governing your nonprofit or public organization is a serious business, but there's no reason why the reports and recommendations that are sent to your board for its monthly or quarterly business meeting shouldn't be explicitly designed for easy reading (or listening) and understanding. One of the top goals of your board's standing committees should be to make sure that anything they send to the board is clear, easily understood, and attractively presented. For example, I recently sat in on the meeting of a social service board's performance monitoring committee, at which the format and content of the monthly financial report were thoroughly discussed, with an eye to making the financial report more user-friendly. Board members had been receiving a multipage financial report chock full of numbers that was extremely difficult to understand and ugly to boot. It could have been designed by a sadist, and was certainly primo reading for a group of masochists.

It didn't take long for committee members to reach agreement with the CEO and chief financial officer on the design of an executive summary that, using bar charts, would compare actual with budgeted expenditures—year-to-date and for the month—by major programmatic and administrative categories. Since some board members felt uncomfortable giving up the detail that they were accustomed to receiving, it was agreed to provide it in an appendix to the report.

## SPICING UP BOARD MEETINGS

CEOs who are willing to don the Chief Theatrical Producer hat can take some simple, inexpensive steps to spice up the regular board meeting agenda. For example, one school district I've worked with regularly rotates school board meetings among the different school buildings in the district, making a point of inviting the parents of children enrolled in the buildings to attend the meetings and conducting a tour of the buildings before convening the board meetings. A local agency serving the blind and visually impaired has built a "Spotlight on the Staff" section into its regular monthly board meeting agenda. Managed by the board's planning and development committee, the spotlight segment has added spice to board meetings by featuring outstanding staff members, who describe their work and respond to board members' questions. The standing committees of a public transportation authority regularly invite outside speakers to make presentations and answer questions during their respective segments of the monthly board meeting. For example, the authority board's external relations committee arranged for the county executive to share her thoughts on the authority's working relationship with the county at a recent board meeting.

## INVOLVING BOARD MEMBERS AS AMBASSADORS

Many board-savvy CEOs encourage their boards' external relations committees to oversee a board speakers bureau that books board members for speaking engagements in such forums as service club luncheons. This is a very effective way of making the governing experience of board members more interesting and enjoyable, just so long as you make sure that your board speakers are well supported in taking on this public relations work. For example, your board ambassadors need to be provided with speaking aids such as a script with pertinent talking points, PowerPoint slides, attractive handouts, and even an opportunity to rehearse in a safe setting (such as an executive team meeting).

Speaking can be an interesting and ego-satisfying experience for board members, as can representing your organization on external task forces and committees. For example, one board member I know recently represented her public transportation authority on the county's economic development task force, which over a period of eight months fashioned recommendations for attracting new business to the community by various means, including featuring the public transportation system in promotional materials. This was more than merely an extra-curricular experience intended to enrich the governing life of a board member, as it turns out, because one of the direct results of the task force's work was wide agreement to support a sales tax increase for the authority.

## STRENGTHENING INTERACTION

Narrowing the distance that separates the people on your board, breaking through unnecessary barriers, and making human connections are important ways to enrich your board members' governing experience and to strengthen your partnership with the board. Board-savvy CEOs know that familiarity breeds not contempt, but mutual understanding and emotional bonding that help cement teamwork and partnership: among board members, between the board and CEO, and between the board and executive team. Knowing someone at a deeper level builds an emotional line of credit that can be drawn on when grappling with thorny issues and dealing with the inevitable stresses and strains involved in high-impact governing.

The savviest CEOs I've worked with over the years have taken advantage of every opportunity to break down interpersonal barriers and strengthen the emotional ties that bind board members more closely together with each other and with the CEO and executive team members. I have seen board-savvy CEOs successfully employ a variety of practical, low-cost techniques over the years for narrowing interpersonal distance. For example, you can take the initiative in orchestrating and facilitating such social interactions as an informal board get-together over lunch or a light supper before the monthly board meeting, periodic receptions, a December holiday party, a summer picnic, a social evening built into the annual strategic work session. And several of my clients have produced a board bio book, consisting of board member photos and biographical sketches. These are all modest steps that don't cost much, but over time experience has proved that they can yield a strong return in terms of board member enjoyment and satisfaction—and ultimately the board-CEO partnership itself.

# KEY #5:
# PUT A WELL-DESIGNED CEO EVALUATION PROCESS IN PLACE

EXPERIENCE HAS TAUGHT ME that there is no tool more powerful than regular, formal board evaluation of CEO performance for maintaining a healthy board-CEO working relationship. Unfortunately, many if not most, nonprofit and public boards do a less than effective job of carrying out their evaluation responsibility. Some boards have been known to leave CEO evaluation to the board chair, thereby abdicating their collective responsibility; others have relied on one of those generic checklists that measure functional competence (for example, assessing how well the CEO handles such executive functions as long-range financial planning and human resource management), while ignoring critical leadership outcomes. And I have even encountered boards that have gone for years without evaluating their CEO's performance, either because they do not recognize the importance of evaluation as a leadership tool, feel uncomfortable judging their CEO, or just plain do not know how to go about evaluating performance.

If you're a really board-savvy CEO, you won't just sit back and wait for your board to decide that it's time to begin evaluating your performance; nor would you just passively go along with whatever process your board (or more likely, a highly vocal member of the board) comes up with. The stakes are too high for such a casual approach, and it's incumbent on you to take the initiative in recommending to your board the major elements of an evaluation process that will strengthen your partnership with the board.

## FEATURES OF A MODEL PROCESS

Although a well-designed CEO evaluation process can be very

helpful in making judgments about the CEO's compensation level, making a very sensible link between performance and financial rewards, the primary objective of the process is to strengthen CEO performance and the CEO's partnership with the board. The following design features are characteristic of highly effective evaluation processes that real-life nonprofit and public boards around the country have put to good use in keeping their partnership with the CEO close, positive, and enduring:

•A board standing committee takes explicit responsibility for adopting the detailed design of the CEO evaluation process—on the recommendation of the CEO—and for conducting the evaluation. If your board is very small (say, fewer than nine members, as is the case with the majority of school boards), then it will make sense for the whole board to conduct the evaluation, sitting as a committee-of-the-whole. Either way, intensive time is set aside to do the evaluation outside of the regular board meeting framework.

•In carrying out the evaluation, the responsible committee employs two sets of criteria for assessing CEO performance:

1. Overall organizational targets, as defined through the operational planning and budget preparation process, and

2. CEO-specific leadership targets that are negotiated with the responsible board committee at the beginning of each new fiscal year (see below).

•The process involves intensive, face-to-face committee-CEO dialogue, making the CEO an active participant in the evaluation and never leaving him or her out of the loop. Issues relating to the board-CEO partnership, no matter how sensitive, are explicitly addressed during this dialogue, which might require two or more committee meetings over a period of weeks. For example, I recently sat in on an evaluation session—one of three that had been scheduled—that focused heavily on the CEO's style of communicating with her board, which had alienated several board members. If this style issue, which would not normally be identified through one of those trivial functional checklists, had been allowed to fester, it might very well have led to an unfortunate parting of the ways, but, fortunately, it was addressed in time to prevent serious damage.

•Going beyond the performance appraisal itself, the evaluation process results in detailed agreement between the committee and CEO on the specific steps that the CEO will take during the coming year to correct performance shortfalls and clear deadlines for each step. For example, the evaluation committee and CEO of a social services agency I worked with a few years ago agreed that the CEO was neglecting her diplomatic role and focusing too much attention on internal administrative matters. She agreed that, beginning in January, she would spend at least half of her time in the external arena, promoting the agency's public image and building stronger working relationships with a list of critical stakeholder organizations they had identified.

•And the committee briefs the full board in executive session, reviewing the evaluation results and the resulting agreement between the committee and CEO on the steps that will be taken to deal with performance issues.

## REAL DRIVER OF THE EVALUATION PROCESS

Board-CEO negotiation of CEO-specific leadership targets is the real driver of an effective evaluation process. In developing this set of targets, the board committee responsible for the evaluation process and the CEO will answer the question: What specific targets should the CEO devote significant individual time and attention to achieving in the coming year? In other words, what will be the CEO's unique value-added to the organization?

The point of negotiating these CEO-specific targets—above and beyond the overall organizational targets related to program implementation, service delivery, finances, administration, and the like, that are established through the annual operational planning/budget process—is to provide your board and CEO with a more finely calibrated instrument to employ in both assessing the CEO's performance and managing the relationship. This is critical to maintaining a healthy partnership for the very simple reason that board-CEO relationships reach the breaking point every day in nonprofit and public organizations that are actually performing well according to the organization-wide performance targets set through the planning process. Countless times over the past twenty-five years, I have seen CEOs receive high marks for overall leadership of their organizations while at the same time running into serious relationship trouble with their boards, over such CEO-specific matters as support for the board in developing its governing capacity, how the external relations role is being divided between the board and CEO, and board-CEO communication.

I want to be clear: I am not suggesting that CEO-specific leadership targets are as important in the grand scheme of things as the bottom-line programmatic and administrative targets that the CEO and senior executives develop through the annual operational planning and budget process and the board ultimately adopts. Nor do I believe that CEO-specific targets need to be uniformly quantitative since that would be unrealistic in the area of CEO leadership. The point is to employ a tool that enables the CEO and board to engage in a creative, detailed discussion about the CEO's leadership role and to decide how to go about assessing

68

CEO leadership in a meaningful fashion, with the ultimate aim of maintaining a close, productive, and healthy partnership.

## PERFORMANCE CATEGORIES

Your board's evaluation committee and CEO reaching agreement on a set of CEO-specific performance targets for the coming year can be a straightforward process. First, they should agree on the categories within which the targets will be developed. Second, the CEO should develop a set of targets in these performance categories. Third, the board evaluation committee and CEO should spend adequate time discussing the targets and then formally adopting them as one of two sets of evaluation criteria (the other set being the overall organizational performance targets set through the planning process).

In my experience, four categories of CEO-specific performance make up a workable framework:

1. **Relating to the board-CEO partnership:** including CEO support for the board in carrying out its governing work; board capacity building; board-CEO communication.

2. **Relating to external relations:** including representation of your organization to the public at large and in particular forums in the community; relationships with particular high-priority external stakeholders; media relations.

3. **Relating to strategic planning/innovation and change:** including how the board will be involved in the innovation and change process; what innovation and change issues and initiatives will receive intensive CEO attention.

4. **Relating to internal management and administration:** specific improvements in internal management and administration that the CEO will focus significant individual time on; the specific issues that the CEO will take the lead in solving.

## CEO PERFORMANCE TARGETS

Looking at these four categories, you can easily see that they provide a workable framework for discussing the CEO's performance targets and for grappling with potential and actual issues that are both pertinent to the board-CEO partnership and that would not be likely to come up in the normal operational planning process of your organization. For example, here are some targets that boards and CEOs have reached agreement on over the years:

Regarding the board-CEO partnership, I, as your CEO, will in the coming year:

> •Make sure that the board's three new standing committees become fully functional.

> •Upgrade my communication with the board by implementing a bi-weekly e-mail update for the board and making sure that I meet with every board member individually for an hour every month.

> •Work closely with the treasurer to improve the monthly financial report, making it easier to understand by adding an executive summary and employing bar charts comparing actual to budgeted expenditures by major functional areas—monthly and year-to-date.

Regarding external relations, I, as your CEO, will in the coming year:

> •Make sure that the board speakers bureau is implemented, ensuring that every board member is booked to speak in at least one community forum every quarter and is provided with an attractive PowerPoint presentation to use in making the presentation.

> •Pay special attention to rebuilding our organization's working relationship with the mayor's office and city

council, by improving communication generally and, more specifically, by making sure that they are regularly briefed on important issues.

•See that our organization finds a seat at the economic development table, specifically that both a board member and I are invited to serve on the newly created Community Economic Development Task Force.

Regarding strategic planning/innovation and change, I, as your CEO, will in the coming year:

•Make sure that staff members are well-represented on the task forces that are being created to come up with change initiatives to address the strategic issues that we identified at the last retreat.

•Play a hands-on role in putting the capital levy steering committee together, making sure that it represents every major sector and key stakeholders in our community and that it is provided with a clear charge and adequate executive support.

In the area of management and administration, I, as CEO, will in the coming year:

•Make sure that the new Director of Contracts Management position is filled with a highly qualified candidate and that new policies and procedures are developed and put into place within six months at the outside.

•Play a hands-on leadership role in addressing the issue of internal morale, making sure that the employee survey that will be conducted in September 2010 indicates significant improvement in every measurement category.

71

Of course, your CEO's specific performance targets in these four important leadership areas will provide a more solid foundation for your board's evaluation of CEO performance to the extent that they can be quantified. Even though this will not always be possible, trying to come up with measurable indicators that the performance promises are being kept will add objectivity to the evaluation process. For example, referring back to the above examples, "Make sure that the board's three new standing committees become fully functional" can be measured by defining what "fully functional" means: Has each committee been thoroughly oriented on its responsibilities? Is each committee meeting at least monthly? Is each committee reporting on its work at regular board meetings?

You will not be surprised to learn that, in my experience, many CEOs will not welcome a dialogue with their board on their CEO-specific leadership targets, viewing it from a traditional defensive perspective as an assault on executive prerogatives. Time and again, when I mention the subject in workshop presentations, I see skeptical looks on several faces in the audience and several hands shoot up to challenge me. The inevitable question goes something like this: "My board's job isn't to do my job! How I use my time doing X, Y, and Z isn't any of their business. I'm paid to be the CEO, I'll do the job my way, and they can just judge the bottom-line results. That's what a board is for. If I get them involved in discussing my detailed leadership work, the next thing I know they'll be sitting in my chair and lobbing commands to my executive team. No thank you!"

My response is a dose of tough love: "I feel your pain, dear colleagues; I know that the idea sends chills up and down your spine. But you've got no choice if you really want to have a strong, mutually satisfying relationship with your board. Reaching detailed agreement with your board on your individual leadership targets is the surest way to avert the kinds of issues that can kill the partnership, no matter how well your organization is performing overall. By participating in such a dialogue, you make it possible to discuss matters, such as your board members' ego satisfaction, that would otherwise fall through the cracks and come back to haunt you. And you also convey your fundamental executive maturity and self-confidence by enabling the dialogue."

In closing, if you're a board-savvy CEO, you'll just make sure it happens—period.

# AFTERWORD

I APPRECIATE YOUR ALLOWING me to be your guide on this brief tour of the board-CEO partnership terrain, and I trust that you've found reading *Building a Rock-Solid Partnership With Your Board* both interesting and informative. Whatever nonprofit or public business you're in—aging, association management, economic development, education, health care, social services or transportation—be assured that you can put the five keys you've just read about to immediate use in building the kind of close, positive and enduring board-CEO partnership that these challenging times demand. There are other partnership-building tools available to you, of course, but real-life experience has taught me that you've got to have these five in your CEO toolkit. I've thoroughly tested them in hundreds of real-life situations over the past quarter century, so you can rely on the fact that they actually work in practice if you're seriously committed to developing a really cohesive board-CEO Strategic Governing Team.

You can't afford to tarry. Putting board-CEO partnership building on the back burner is likely to come at a forbiddingly high cost—a board that doesn't come to grips with the highest stakes issues facing your organization; a dysfunctional board-CEO working relationship that demoralizes staff and tarnishes your organization's image; and, ultimately, failure to translate your organization's vision into reality. To be honest, I can't promise that the partnership-building path you travel will be uniformly smooth; you'll likely encounter potholes and road blocks aplenty along the way. But I can promise that if you are determined to put the five keys that I describe in this guidebook to work in your organization— and you are willing to commit the requisite time and attention to the task—you'll succeed in building the kind of board-CEO partnership that the times demand.

# ABOUT THE AUTHOR

DOUG EADIE IS THE FOUNDER and president of Doug Eadie & Company, a firm that specializes in building governing board leadership capacity and strengthening the board-CEO partnership. Over the past twenty-five years, Doug has worked with more than 500 public and nonprofit organizations.

He is the author of seventeen other books on nonprofit leadership, including *Meeting the Governing Challenge, High-Impact Governing in a Nutshell* and *Extraordinary Board Leadership*. Before founding his consulting practice, Doug held several senior positions in the public and nonprofit sectors. He is a Phi Beta Kappa graduate of the University of Illinois at Urbana and received his master of science in management degree from the Weatherhead School at Case Western Reserve University.

## OTHER BOOKS BY DOUG EADIE

*Extraordinary Board Leadership (Second Edition).* Jones and Bartlett, Sudbury, Massachusetts, 2008.

*Meeting the Governing Challenge.* Governance Edge, Oldsmar, Florida, 2007.

*Five Habits of High-Impact School Boards.* Roman & Littlefield Education, Lanhan, Maryland, 2005.

*High-Impact Governing in a Nutshell.* ASAE, Washington, DC, 2004.

*Eight Keys to an Extraordinary Board-Superintendent Partnership.* Roman & Littlefield Education, Lanham, Maryland, 2003.

*The Board-Savvy Superintendent* (with Paul Houston). Roman & Littlefield Education, Lanham, Maryland, 2002.

*The Extraordinary CEO in Public Transportation.* APTA, Washington, DC, 2000.

*The Extraordinary CEO.* ASAE, Washington, DC, 1999.

*Changing By Design.* Jossey-Bass, San Francisco, 1997.

*Boards That Work.* ASAE, Washington, DC, 1994.

Visit www.DougEadie.com for more information on books, CDs, and web-based training from Doug Eadie & Company.

Breinigsville, PA USA
09 March 2010
233894BV00002B/12/P